Published 2005
by

Smokestack Books
PO Box 408, Middlesbrough TS5 6WA
Tel : 01642 813997
e-mail : info@smokestack-books.co.uk
www.smokestack-books.co.uk

Photography by Ivan Coleman

Design and print by
James Cianciaruso
j.cianciaruso@ntlworld.com

ISBN 0-9548691-4-1

Smokestack Books
gratefully acknowledges the support of
Middlesbrough Borough Council
and Arts Council North East.

Smokestack Books is a member of
Independent Northern Publishers
www.northernpublishers.co.uk

Lightyear

poems by Alison Fell photographs by Ivan Coleman

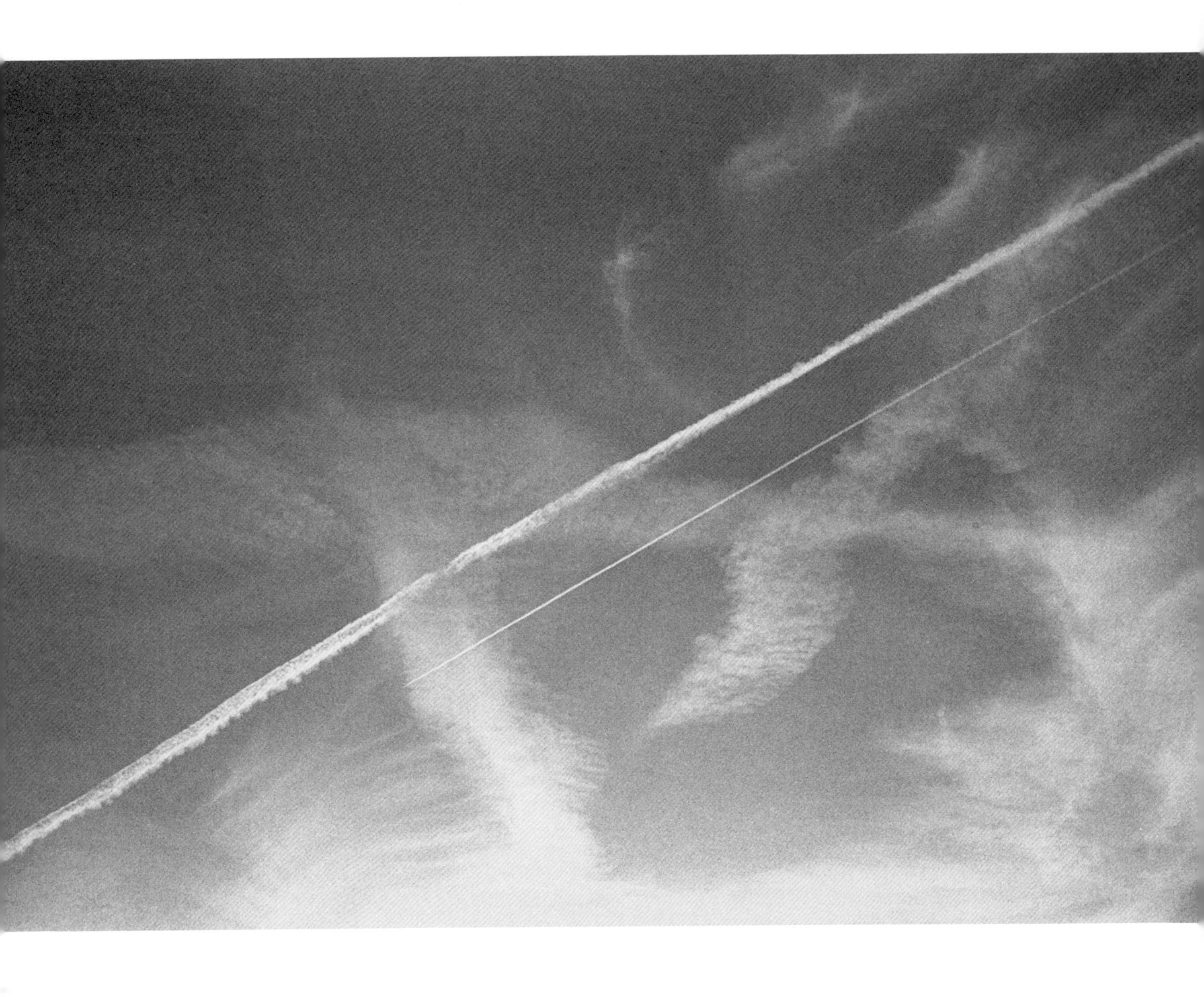

October

1

Above the church spire, twin lengths
of tie-dyed sky
joined by a vertical zip:

the plane climbs, clinks like a piggy-
bank, talking the language
of money.

Down here, the inaudible murmur
of the deer and the other animals.

The lawns have demanded to be clipped.

A boy rubs from his eyes the shadow
that sticks to his ball
like a terrifying bedtime story.

Goose-cries now
like a trashy radio left on loud
but distantly.

2

The poplar is the dark star
of the garden.

People with their jackets
in their hands
pass by slowly.

First red nudge of berries
on the rowan:

luxurious jottings.

The rowan picks up her pen,
aims herself at nothing.

She decides to glisten.
Her hair and her statements
decide to glisten.

3

The chestnuts are stout fair fellows
lolling in the fallen leaves -

time to be foreign again,
bury all gold for the look
and the shine of it.

I position myself on the café terrace,
half-beast, book half-open
on the sugared table.

Birds swift as sleet on a taxing
wind: each soaked rose
has been written and rewritten.

Spilt milk runs on the flagstones
with the rain.

Old letters are asking
to talk to me.

Time to submit to dismemberment,
and the great intermediary
silences, like the sea's.

4

Listening from the park
you can hear sky's

dinning grey
the more acutely

when a butterfly's
white quiet cuts across

the grumble
like a feather of

the winter your next
inaudible outbreath

will surely
loosen, make possible.

5

(After J-F. Lyotard)

Beyond black trees the sky's
exorbitant sunset
full of light and death.

The sky looking back at its life-
line lowers its eyelids
and laughs at business:

lines of luck or misfortune,
sunstripes painted on the sea
advancing and receding.

The sky is not yet profitable.
Its floods of gold follow
Koranic laws, prohibit usury.

Now dull, now shrill, like the pebbles
crying out to the tide to tumble
them again, again,

now shedding a shower of ash leaves
from its Great Ephemeral Skin,

now standing in for a brand new
fragment of the beautiful

6

And sometimes the shoulders
of the sky peaked up and dark
like hanging bats

as if in anger or the fading
hope of wings.

The Jesuits and not the crows
invented sophistry:

these boys
with their pussy-willow
cheeks and old men's hands,

ridged nails, and ravaged
knowing skin.

Job lied. The light of God
is constant.

Fire is the proof, the apparent
simplicity of the thing.

Thumbnail always at the teeth,
the wounds not crossing
the throat's border:

all the questions unasked
of the Great Zero,

all of winter's hungers that won't
come clean.

1 November

Clang of a school bell: the signal
which starts up the propellors of the leaves,

the driven leaves which savagely
attack the bus windows.

Bus full of bonnets and sneezes.

It's a small and warlike time
easily misunderstood,

bullied from the North, the South,
hard to bless it or find excuses.

They say you can't teach anyone
anything on afternoons like these:

everyone thinking they're a verb like a comet,
everyone wanting to be everywhere, like leaves.

2

If the clocks are dejected it's because
the sunflowers turn their backs
on them, won't answer to their names.

Anyone can see how wrinkled
the trees are, like the mirror
you could strangle first thing.

Even the one we call the willow
has two faces, one pressed thinly
to the inviolable trunk like a lightning-

conductor, the other a flamenco-flounce
the whorish wind describes:

summer's last tantrum, the air
charged in the margins.

Who can tell wrong from right
with any confidence, or earth
the currents of excess;

who shall be Mother, hemming up
the darkness with her little pins?

3

November does not want us
to talk about him.

We wear brown felted horns
and quiet boots,

maintain camouflage,

do nothing to call up
the desire of the dark.

The bed has been sharpened:

under the black anchored sheet
of the forest we carry
the moon in our mouths.

We show no light
divulge no itinerary,

tell no one it is winter's
beast that crawls on its belly
through the wicker city.

4

Nothing you can say will make
any difference,

though you may wait, cold
at heart, still hoping for
ridiculous favours.

Think of the Last Emperor,
a baby bald as the land

with his abacus and the parallel
furrows of his brow,

massed wind-banners of red
silk, of sand,

a weak sun deciphering
the skinny portents of birds

and the water-carriers
like theorems

kowtowing
to the little lord
of the terrible acres.

5

The moon so commanding
and full, like a general,
shakes us from our insect sleep,

for are we not his loft
of apples to be turned about
so none will rot?

Deep in the night-
house we roll sideways
to air our sheets of straw,

a reddening herd,
stoked by the fires
of talk and silence, singing

our apple-song, convivial
to the core.

6

What's green is going, taking
with it the last hiding-places
of the light, its spills
and splashes.

The trunk of the one wild cherry
ink black, like the swan's neck,
its leaves sharp scarlet beaks.

The land's flayed bare by its reckonings
with the century -

torn off a strip,
like the sod that Private Harry Farr
stops under.

The moon pins its white square
of flannel over the heart.

Dawn drips its slate-light
across the field,

scratches another name
on its sum of wonders.

(Harry Farr was a young Yorkshire soldier
shot in Flanders for so-called desertion)

December

1

In the ghost-mist above the rooftops
planes stalk one another

in spirals, punctilious,
like the rakings of a sand-garden

in which someone might sit
and count his blessings.

Some bits of luck these last
few days: ground has a good

feel to the heels, hair
likes to crouch under its hat,

fingertips nest nicely
in their woollen gloves.

It's the nose's luck to be
stuck so firmly to a face,

it's the mind's luck to live
in the limitless house of the head.

2

Bruised airflow from the north:
the moon skids madly
on its rink of clouds.

December seen, unseen,
that trip to transparent places.

Cold, cold the inside of the night
when her lover leaves her skin,

the door of the dawn worn thin
from so much knocking.

Ikon colours: low down between
the tree-trunks sun peeling

off the sky like gold leaf
as the old light wheels itself in.

3

White grass, white ironed star
of the sycamore.

On the pond-ice the geese
land awkwardly, like armchairs.

Even for the city bird
starvation becomes a factor:

the poor one
and the rich, the gangster gull,

the urgent blackbird prising up
a cardboard crust of leaves,

the pigeon
tinsel-throated in its glamour.

Heat steams
from the funnels of the houses

whose hearts will winter
elsewhere.

In the dark meltwater of their wake
the birds,

forgotten like the dead,
scavenging and diving.

4

The poems take exception to the rain.
They complain of their ankle-joints,
their elbows.

They reserve the right
not to be relied upon.

They put on weight,
They hoard their sleep
like currency -

not a crumb or a word
let slip, not a coin
in the collecting-plate.

Under the Christmas tree they lie
immobile, with their travellers' eyes.

When the day drowns them out
they look to the merciful night,

Night that takes the form of a train
crossing a forest,

shaking snow-pillows
from the silent branches.

5

The saints on tip-toe
shiver round the spire.

The winter church waits
for its worshippers,

for the wick to be dipped
in the tallow

and the wax tears
to drip on the altar-cloth.

Lower than the lids of the sun
the seagulls circle,

their white bodies heavy
with the scent of snow.

The leaves lie down
on their mattress of bones;

the roses leafless now,
indelible as bloodstains.

The holly carnivorous
in its green lair,

rough-tongued, like my poems
at the year's

end, fattening
for the slaughter.

January

1

Smoke-tailed on the farthest
whisker of a branch

squirrels move like that fast riffle
the cardsharps call a waterfall

or maybe a cascade: fifty two
frames a second. They exist in light
no longer than ghosts do.

At that height, that speed,
their shadows dissipate like wisdom.

Weightless days fill me
with daring: death
gives good odds for once,

my pen turns gambler, throws down
black words like clubs.

2

The blackest of blacks
is the rock at the mist's edge.

The whitest of whites is the fleece
of the burn in spate.

At Hell's Ghyll, the waterfall
blown up like the wide
folds of a skirt,

the weir awash, the dyke
slippery.

Pocketfuls of rain, rain
interfering like thoughts:

the rowan is the truest tree,
she wakes before the birch,

the queen of reds is the wet
russet of the winter bracken.

3

still tree
stretched tree
tree breasting a squall
tree regrouping
tree fingering a hill

tree-shadow on the mist above the moor
tree rain-blind against glass
tree with its hands flying
to its mouth

tree-branch whipping
a sky sullen as youth
tree-branch fallen in the garth

tree-log drying
at the fireside
tree-log knitting its red-and-black
patchwork in the hearth
tree-log whistling its psalm
of surrender

tree-log hollowing
tree-boat borne
on the yellow sails of the flames

funeral-boat whose tiller the axe
leans by the open door

4

Green lichen on the boulders
of the garth.

I make the stock for soup
and stew the apricots, placate

the starveling year that creeps out
from the cracks and slippage
of the clouds.

Good luck be on this hearth:
coal is for warmth
and bread for plenty,

red onions chopped in rings
with parsnip roots
and parsley stalks.

Enter the alchemist.

A black hat runs on the river-
bank like a wheel,

wind bursting like lava from the fell's
throat, and the New Year's grim

knock at the gate

5

Off Lindisfarne
the waves shiver like monks
at their ablutions.

Under high horizontals
of ice-cloud, the sky
scrubbed clean as a dairy.

The train darts north,
hungry as a tongue.

Only the exile longs for
the words to name a country:

either live it or learn,
at a bare table,

ancestral silence, like a rumble
deep in the loch’s throat,

the forgotten song
of the curling-stone,

the snow slipping like white meat
from the bones of the mountain.

6

January gives me a dark eye
and a light,

one patched like a pirate,
obliged to look in,

the other squinting out at the park
like a spring animal.

What my dark eye knows
is the blind underbelly
of the turf,

the brown dog
in the dream that defies gravity,

and, in the premature dusk,
Concorde swooping down from the storm-cloud,
not silver for once

but tar-black, lucid
as a galleon in the hieratic spread
of its sails.

February

1

Crow's scissor-beak cawing
in a dead elm:

dressmaker crow
which mends nothing,

rips the light raw,

makes the trusting trees
wait and wait for renovation.

2

A story from Yakutsk:
if you shout to a lover
in February
across the Lena river
and he can't hear you,
it's because the words have frozen
solid on the vast Siberian air.

Go back there in spring,
when the plum-blossom
is ice-white on the tow-
path, and you will hear the same
words whisper as they thaw:

the drip of winter's discourse,
melting endearments,
his half-forgotten name.

3

Monotonous, like the rain
on the park

the woman from Sri Lanka
rocks on the verandah,

her pamphlet thumbed thin
as her glove -

The Mercy of God:

his quaint cross glowing with light,
his arms outstretched, his robe
white as goose-feathers.

Her moving finger marks
the place of faith,
her prayer chanted sotto voce:

the hard handiwork
of the heart - love
and more love till the stone
surrenders.

4

Still-crumpled spring
with its birdseed blossom,

plywood clouds
secured by unseen props,

and sudden sun, like a spotlight
swivelled on the audience.

Glass birds wink
from a manufactured landscape.

Night flows nowhere,
no kind of understanding grows.

5

Of course it is meant for me -
this little coast house
built on green stilts,
salt-faced, white as a snowdrop.
Unlike an apartment it starts
at the ground and grows up;

the floors unfold in the way
of mountain ranges, at the pace
of heartbeat or footstep, revealing
their slow geography.

It takes time to discover
every bud and branch,
every door that stands wide open,
every balcony that flowers
only for a day.

Wind engineered this house.
When the tide washes
through the mesh of its roots,

seals flow from their dark bay
in the pantry,
flippered and footloose,
their eyes a soft affront
to history,

their silent amniotic language
guiding me back to the sea.

March

1

The invisible hearse of the wind
drives you back to the kerb to stand
stock still while it passes.

The clouds convulsive, plumed like horses.

Who lies shoeless in that satin place,
silent as a bat-box in broad daylight
with a black hole for words,

his rouged face pillowed and put to rights?

The wind comes commonsensical
with its juggernaut song of cause and effect,

as if to say that rage, like sorrow, is the wrong way
of regarding him.

In the vacuum of the streets only rhythm
remains - the tap-dance of empty chairs
on a balcony, the archaic drumbeat of shutters,

white luggage of bone-dust or blossom.

2

Each thing you look at
makes up a history
that one day will be yours.

One look infuses the atom with energy,
unleashes a flurry of colours
in the world's flesh.

Lips also have a way
of watching but it is hungrier
and bruises things:

the mountains are milked dry
like breasts, weighed down
by your amazement.

Things fold in like wings:
the clenched bud furiously
guards its privacy,

the pheasant, hearing
the music of foxes,
shies away.

3

All winter the sun in sackcloth
and we in our merits,
shivering.

The moths of cold have nibbled
at our faces,

we scratch our matchstick days
on the wall.

The boat of the north
chimes out on the breaking ice.

Bright rain sudden
on the stones like a bell
or a pardon.

The plum blossom
tries out its wings;

the grey wind, bewildered,
looks on
at its offspring.

4

The wind drops: sun
for the first time feels
my face.

The park is pruned and proud
and ready for the thumbprint
of the light.

We breathe the same breath,
the same expectation
of green heat,

while down in the dark the compost
does its secret worry-work.

Beware the anniversaries
of March, the grey gods fingering
their invisible chimneys.

The road burns in the grass.
The doors of the house pinch
when the smear of sunset passes.

5

Can't even dream about him,
I am ill
from a fear of doing ill.

Ill with loudness,
like a hawthorn tree full
and whistling with sparrows.

Ill with wriggling, like the legless
sac of a doodlebug
exciting the amoral air.

Ill as he might have been
on the night-flight
back from Dresden.1945,

that spring when I turned boneless
with delight at everything
below and above me.

Father.
In my mouth the word
has the silent mould of a zoo-
animal, a chimpanzee,
or a zebra set free
by the firestorm.

Like a continent waiting
for forgiveness, I did not know
what shape I should be in -

a belonging in a black pram,
daffodil face, noun
without agency.

He had his oiled overalls
and his orders,
his memories of amputees

and mother, waiting day
after day at the barbed wire,
dressed like a separation.

April

1

When green breathes out
the first chalk-monsters
appear on the pavements.

Whites compare force-fields:
the blackthorn snowy,
the narcissus buttery.

On the bare mast of a crab-apple
a chaffinch buffs its breast
against the blue,
strikes the first spark.

Within a week the fuse is lit -

the church spire flattens iself
on its belly against the blast;

in the shellholes of the road
puddles open in which the brand new
bulky treetops stalk you,
swaying like tanks

2

Trezelah comes when I'm lonely
over the ivy-wall
after the storm.

Cornish cat on loan from a painter,
with her ultramarine purr
and her yawn.

Clear-weather cat
curled like a sun-snail
on my writing-arm.

Dandelion-eyed, watching
for words or the squalls
moving in from the headland.

Her fur cirrus-striped,
colour of driftwood
and coal-smoke.

Her whiskers a clock-face
commanding the hours
of the harbour:

the ship of Art will dock
at her discretion
and the tide's.

3

The sea withdraws from me.
The sea purses her lips together
and whistles like a shell.

The sea leaves me and goes
to the altar with the bridegroom
who deserves her.

Where the sea was
is a dark room of rubble
the tears step in saltily
to refill.

The sea has thrown me
her bouquet of white foam -

her petals pale as memory,
like a million refugees

whispering to one another
across the tides of wind.

4

In the game that begins again
you cannot be unpartnered.

Tin is my name, my note
abandonment,

even the chestnut wears the red
shoes that stand in for my shame.

The sun weaves its wickerwork
on the water: spring's charmed
spine uncoils like smoke.

The sky is that blue ballroom
where first we met.

(Dance the only glove
that ever truly fitted me;

even the little mermaid
has her knives,
her entrance fee)

5

Water black as a bowl of grapes
into which the shining night imports
its pin-head moons.

From her dark embrace with the mirror,
mother swims up to meet me,

many-nippled, tufts of leopard-fur
sewn into the skin of her cheeks,

suit-pockets like seal-ears
of black velvet.

Down in her water-programme
she will play with me
for ages before she kills me:

twisted love, like a voice
arguing from the sea.

6

Clean morning spruces
the night's wet grass:

greens grow into their different
darknesses.

The park is a green pail
frothed with white geese.

Deer ring the abrupt
shade of the chestnut,
nose to tail.

Summer is the thing we think about,
blue without border-posts,

red crab-boat
and sea-smell,
our bare feet out to air like buds,

the fleet far out
from the coast,

the gorse on the wall,
golden and privileged.

Also of the above named
JEREMIAH BILLENNESS

May

1

Mostly I want to put my best
foot forward, to place a future
under construction.

The sky is bright and stretched
like a balloon, the ground
bleeding.

Coins of clover scattered
on a spendthrift green;

my feet are my fundaments,
collapsing.

That step, however tentative,
still tramples on you.

piano piano piano

The earth is a grave
on which nettles grow
tall as crutches.

Boneless light, a blur
of baking trees.

2

The smell of the rain,
the saucer skirts of the hawthorn
heavy with it.

In her copse Madam Rhododendron -
that import of dyed and faded silks -
holds court, scrubbed pink
and ready in her sleeves and layers,

attended to by lesser ladies:
the birch and lime, the blue willow
with its pattern of flight.

The shape of her under birds,
bent forward by her bulk
of fabrics,
as if crossing the humped bridge,
taking the ghost road into exile.

The cuckold chestnut wears
white horns for her;
the canal is a lake on which blossom-
boats are driven like ripples.

3

The doorways all written in bluebells,
drooping with green branches,
tell a story that is liminal.

The teenagers sly-eyed on cider,
the Neolithic reek of laughter,
the raucous squeal of the accordion.

Black as creosote, the forensic skirt
of the Obby Oss circles like a sawblade
or a shadow of the sun.

Mayhem is the rule,
the only guarantee of growth.
Lie down with her in the slaughter-
house, where the stone seed
passes secretly from mouth to mouth.

On the threshold the butcher
dances with his cleaver,
while the cows turn back to their salt-lick,
for beasts know nothing of merriment,
and less of what humans call animal -

the dead beat of the sacrificial drum,
how a whole village can go on heat,
or how its helpless feet are factories
for following a memory
of beef and blood, something sloe-black,
unseen, expelled like an afterbirth.

4

The terrier is barking at the Chinese bag,
the way it crouches on the grass
at the woman's feet.

He is worried about the colours,
colours no self-respecting dog has ever seen -
orange coat appliquéd with blue

and green chrysanthemums, also the sheen
of the satin and the pink upright ears
of the handles -

a breed which belongs in no English park,
brick-shaped, no tail to wag,
an immigrant

which bares its rhinestone teeth
and won't retreat.

5

The following were not allowed in the house:
A lone glove, dropped.
The new moon's crescent glimpsed in the mirror.
The sky-spars of an open umbrella.

There was also the rubric of May
and its blossoms. Granny barred the door
against the hawthorn and the sloe,
even the rowan with its friendly acrid smell of underwear,

so that Bride the white goddess
could not dance herself in from the moor,
or too much beauty break and enter
her winter store of darkness.

6

If you were to think of painting May
you would think of a locus of appearances -
the nature-goddess yanked from the soil
like a snake from its hole and shaping herself

as a tortoise or a sheaf of barley.

You would look with the clear eye
of Aphrodite *Kyanopeis* at her washing-day
and see the starched iris, the hyacinth,
the sickle-blade of every stainless shadow,

and you would dream of a going-into-blue,
into the stippled brushwork of the wistaria
and the blue glaze of the sky where the bees meet,

then also of its exact golden opposite,

for honey is the colour of sun through eyelids
and above all the pure food of the Oracle,
transparent as the truth her handmaids the *Melissae*

etch on the air by their way-of-buzzing,
their way-of-flying.

June

1

This must be the month when Mercury started it,
tongue in cheek, stirring his sky-pot,
scattering the winged languages.

First, the pictograph with its chiselled petals,
then its linear equivalent, syllabic -
the exact whistlestop shape of a swallow.

Philology: How sound falls in love with script.

What I have to put my mind to
is June's own rain-noise,
the talk that drowns out the traffic.

Fricatives and plosives, tree-language
learned in the schoolroom of wind.

Translations from the rose-garden,
the half million sweet nothings you can't make out.

Bird-gossip,
blown husks like ripped envelopes,
rowan-flowers white as folded-open letters.

And that black man
under the branch stock still with his ear
to the air and its underwater wash of shadows.

2

Remember the tinkers' camp
by the river-road: bent birches
lashed to make a bower, the tarpaulin
long gone, and the unsheltered
eyes of the children.

The cooking fire's a vestige - ring
of black stones, soaked ash,
cruel cans burnt or rusted.

The birds distinctly silent,
and the raspberries stripped from the soaked
clearing: nothing but bare white hulls.

Did they whistle, were they
folk at all, did they make a tune
strangely by the waterfall,
did the deep fish die of it?

Come away from their carborundum
stone, their constant smell
of wicked weather,
come away to the house where
our mother and our father are.

Faces of steam at the night window,
sharp sharp their scissors
at the lamplight-ribbons of the door.

Dark, like a magpie, knows
its lawless nest, its hidey-hole
for stolen safety pins.

Under our sleeping lids
who do those eyes belong to,
and those migrant dreams?

We change and must not,
drink a little air, and splay
forbidden faces to the rain.

Our beds are broken furze
and foxglove, our horses
driven on and on -

Such a lesson the dogs
of the field will teach us,
if we tarry long.

3

And the breasts and the simple-
minded breezes and the girls unbounded,
passing under the shadows,
and the women in *chadoor* come out to play.

The squeak of a yellow trike:
a manless park.

Kings with crusader-flags, the stay-
at-homes are glued to the footie.

The cellphone silent and the cypress,
and the coronetted march of roses.

The kids looking forward
to Jubilee Day, and up and around
at the incontrovertibly queenly sky,
a blue falling-away.

4

Little horse-girls,
print-frock palominos
spanking their own rumps,
their blond tails flat out
behind them on the bracken-track.

The yellow horse-adder, hoofless,
basks unseen at the fork.

Later, the story goes, they stumbled
on him, braked and skidded, white-
eyed, pawing at the turf.

In the hot-damp stink of the bracken-hut
adders coil themselves like rag-rugs,

but the light of the North
is long and lovely,
and Mother has made fairy-cakes
for a midsummer birthday.

Back at the ranch the red jelly
quivers in its rubber skin.

Dolly will not mind it,
spooned on her plastic saucer:

The house can be hers, its little sink
and draining-board, its empty
hearth, the inside
secrets of its seams.

That tiny cardboard dark
is nothing we need.

No bedtime for us, no slithering dreams -

instead, short nights,
the sky for kith and kin,
a stable, speed.

5

Well north of the young Tay
and its tractors, the birches shimmer
in their shapes of air
and all the remembered moors
badger at the train.

Once I was six, escaping somewhere,
to Siberia perhaps, or
the Sea of Japan.

Night over Bohespic, the uprooted
stars fleeing behind the open back
of the van.

Here is the flight-plan
of the future: the cockpit,
the Samurai pilot in shirtsleeves and a red head-band,
plotting his diamond grid across the stratocirrus.

Always it's the story of air
and how to sail on it:
the biography of the birch,
its nimbleness, its sleight of soul,
its silver variants.

Midges at their cat's cradle
above the trout-pool.

Out of layered cloud
comes a single fin of light.

July

1

In the valley they have locked
their windows against the night forest
and its mist-wraiths:

les âmes des trépassés

for always there's the effort
of forgetting what mountains
are made for:

the manufacture of clouds,
the carding and combing of slipstreams.

An efficiency against which
words are weightless
and dreaming, like snow.

Then sometimes the stillness
is so sheer, tall blue bales of it
stacked up by the morning,

that the mountain makes no sense
but some symmetry we know
we lack

and the climbers come down
quietly through the cairn-fields,
full of fear and beauty

2

In the hot night of the city
noise divines a vacuum,
eddies in, eager,
through the open ducts
of the windows.

Slap of sea-traffic
at the heels of the wardrobe,
then waist-high, undulating
like a tablecloth.

Dust-cries drown in the trees.
The moon's drum beats
under the bedcovers.

The face of the noise,
its nose a Colossus
at the flung-open windows,

its black marble eye
pitiless.

Its nostril inhales,
exhales

the din of the streets,
the turbulence of the air
and its opportunities.

3

In my dream I was telling you,
You've got to go to Onion Square,
it's in Soho, there a secret garden
there, a place where people go
to worship tears; they slip away
at lunchtime or from bars.

The sadness of an onion is generous
and spreads; it reeks of the healthy
dark that fattened it with fluids.

Its cult is global, non-denominational,
an antidote to viruses like bigotry.
You'll need a knife; apart from that
there's precious little ceremony.

4

When they came back from the glacier
they said they had seen
a great ice-bed in the grotto
with ice-pillows plumped up
nicely on the counterpane.

There was a drip drip
from the picture-rail
and the rocking-chair, and a real
warm-blooded St. Bernard
melting the slushy shape of its tail
on the hearth rug.

And they thought there should have been
an ice-mother, lace-apronned,
with a mop and pail,
ice-tulips in an altered vase,
a cryogenic infant, even,
straining on its potty,

and maybe, through the thinning blue sheen
of the ceiling, ice-birds impermanent
as contrails, chiselling across
the high hot July afternoon.

5

After Eluard

Now he is the ghost of a pigeon,
the terracotta berries beginning
as a blush.

The sun stands on his lids,
and his hair is the grey wing
of my hair,

colour of mica and shovels.

In the continent of light
or the continent of darkness
he does not let me sleep.

Even with his sockets open
to the sky his dreams dazzzle.

The dust of his thousand eyes
winking on the wind like pollen:

du Tausendschon

Increments love uncovers
with her sable brush.

Air-traffic: the bees and I
blinded and colliding.

6

Let the sun work for a living
while we, like toddlers, bare-legged,
try out our laughter.

In blue canvas shoes with buckles,
experiment with slope, acceleration,
falling into a rosebed.

Assess the potential of park bench,
sandpit, an appropriate sparrow, pin
them to the concept of mirth.

For already some have begun
to turn their backs on it -

that pale girl in a sun-hat
like a bucket, steering her purposeful
doll's pram dead straight, white-knuckled,

her dress Amish, her frown
ankle-length, deliberate.

August

1

Rowing backwards to Albania

Don't talk to me about the Animus
here in Logos, where the word
is made flesh.

Just give me a little boat
with the power of ten horses
that can ride like a flea
on the glittering pelt
of the Ionian.

Looked at from the balcony
you'd say it was too muscular a sea
for women to sail on -

each boat has its man
at the helm, the wife with the picnic-
hamper, or the mistress posing
in the prow.

We knew we were frail: each crashing
of hull against wave was a slap
on the haunch of the black bull
under us, that midnight thing;

the outboard was our own
fine slice of thunder.

I have been
a serious threat to swimmers.
I have shouted sorry in five languages:
scusi pardon signomi entschuldigung

We blamed ourselves, of course,
when the engine failed us -
so far out
and stricken into silence -

for a small boat
it had borne its load bravely
blonde heads, blonde heels,
the rest.

The sea has undressed
others before us,
the little silver fish have pecked
at freckled Viking meat.

At times like this a girl should
wave the red petticoat,
as Maggie said,
but I'm the resourceful sort,
I thought I knew best.

For oars there were olive-boughs,
salt-soaked, their dead weight
booting us stupidly north.
I have been brute mariner,
idiot militia.
I have locked horns
with the black-browed storm
and the deepest intentions of the sea;

I have faced the wrong way
and rowed backwards to Albania,
for in my mind's eye
the indelible helmsman
always faced the prow.

The waves are women whose white lips
are still strange to us;
their curl is sardonic:
the boats, the oars,
they take for toothpicks.

Hard their limestone hearts,
harder than green lemons,
their fingernails bright as needles
stitching the seam of the sea
to the shore.

I am learning how to throttle back
and idle in to port.
Each touch on the tiller
carves a lucid arc,

Each throw of the anchor
becomes me.

Hand over hand,
like a rope or a net
hauled up,
I am plaiting the waves
into my hair,

I am learning the art
of suave arrival.

2

You are what you eat

Below us, a taverna
where the fish cry out nightly
in their savage battle with the cats.

The hooks of their bones
and their little eyes so very
attached to what eats them.

At lunchtime they sunbathe
on the greased white plates
six feet or less from the sea.

When the sun's eyes are shut
the water-rats skulk,
liverish, along the shore.

The cats in the morning
are tongueless from licking:
80% fish. Scales. Gills.
Breathing the blissful rancid water.

Their tadpole paws paddle them
darkly across the Strait.

They are lost and slender
as black canoes, their snouts
and claws redundant,

only the quick economical
flick of their tails.

The sea has designs on them,
the sea who woke complaining
of the blue spines dragged
from the dustbins.

What will they do
with the urgent instruction to dive?

3

The dirt, the dope, the delinquent heat,
the trashed bus stop, the rap
about police records and air-pistols.

We've got used to having the sun on tap,
can't see what we have, only the deficit:

summer going down, but not without a fight.

When the trees stand still and concentrate,
the noise of their boiling August
drowns us out - the headachey hiss
of pressure-valves, the spit of blue ink
escaping like sap.

4

Nothing on earth that is not
My doing - the dolphin
breasting the waves, the smiling
swordfish, the altostratus, already
a day old, into which I launch
my pelicans and plovers -

yet from the beginning
they have been exactly themselves,
so very busy becoming
that their gaze annihilates.

The young sea learning its laws
looks to Me for what is fathomless;
to the birds I am beaked,
feathered, dancing on gold air.

The hares see Me four-pawed
and furred, exaggerate my ears;
the fishes, monomaniacal, discern
a dorsal fin in the floating
folds of My cloak.

My aspect is partial, skylit,
mirroring but unmirrored -

in the congregations of the newly-
made, no one stands on two
true legs to recognise his like
and cross-examine it.
(I know I will forget all this,
claim them, in My pride,
My loneliness)

5

Chateau de Lavigny

All night the clocks
of three churches
argue about the hour

and in the morning,
sous le cerisier,

pawprints mark the moon-
light dance of the muskrats
on my writing table

September

1

Autumn eradicated from the year
like a faithless ex torn
from a wedding photograph.

The calendar, the clock itself
fixated, watching the replay over and over,
just to be with them.

The game digital and repeatable:

addicts of pleasure
v
addicts of paradise

In the supreme court of symbols,
claim and counter-claim:

Money is only the stupid form
of love, it doesn't compare
with the brilliance of wickedness.

Because anything is better than the sky's
emptiness, the city rewritten, still
as the desert acres of the moon,

the firemen, calloused and loved,
will press the bell for God and country
and the market will begin.

2
At Aberdaron

You come over the brow of the hill
and it hits you -
how the village makes no plan
for its placement, how the fleece-
coloured houses steam and snuggle.

Beyond the river, though,
where the church is,
the headland has a grim tilt to it
and the gravestones face east
by the compass, their black backs
turned to you.

I wouldn't like to be the one who,
lacking some old and proper instinct,
ruled that the soul stops here
at the strict black slate of Bethesda
with the door closed tight
on the westernmost, the uttermost,

who decreed that the terraced dead
had better be curtailed.

There's a parliament of snails
on Richard Evans' stone, well-sheltered
to the leeward. Like the elders

and the others they have agreed
to outlaw the spasms of the sky
and its vacancies.

I think Richard sits at a cold hearth,
his puzzled eyes trained east
on the wrong window,
the one that points to the past
with its razzle-dazzle of birthdays,
its odd annunciatory light,

snails in his parlour and the feeling
that he should long since have set out,
that it is more fitting
to follow the trail of the setting sun
and go the silver way of the sea
with the moon on it: a swift
wise scattering.

3

Saddle-brown squalls and then
the surprise of the sun hotly in
you like a lover.

Heart-weather
of sharp fuschia shadows,

the slow siege of September snails,
patient on their single sucking hooves.

Hot drum of the hedge
and the blackberry glitter of flies.

High up, there's a ruined
cake of a castle, dainty
on its doily cloud.

All the wet benches are catastrophists,
remembering dead kith and kin.

Me, I beat through the ramshackle
bracken, impatient, like trains
or those midge-thoughts of winter
that die spiralling.

Rattle of rain on the beech-wood,
as down the mulched tunnel
to the china bright bluff of the sea
the little horse of impulse goes
rocketing, riderless.

4

September 1620. So committed now,
cutting the apron-strings, remembering
great efforts and crowds.
The quest! The quest!

Consigning the shrinking shores to hell
and the marshy clouds of the motherland.

Certainty. The one reward of the righteous.

Exile has as many gauges as rope
and tugs or slackens
with the tide. How loud
the little voice of expectancy when nothing is
as you expected it to be.

Disappointment is the eel in the eye
of paradise, the threadworm wriggle
of handkerchiefs.

England's farewell on Newlyn Quay:
the beat of the bare-knuckled waves
on the hull, crosspatch sound of the gull
above the last landfall of the Mayflower

before she sailed out past the buoy
and the west to the Americas.

5

Lightning, like a drunk, has no memory.
The axe in its eye - the double-bladed *labrys*
that splits the Cretan sky -
could swing at you not twice
but seven times.

(I'm thinking of that forester in Idaho
who set the record)

keravnovolimeni - literally,
struck by a lightning-bullet.

They say the odds are always even,
but how do they explain affinity,
that recognising heat?

As if some fuddled Alpha-brain,
detecting a history of static surge,
let loose with love its heavy light,
its clumsy arsenal of ions:

the black thunder-hooves of the bull-charge,
and those sharp white horns
you may or may not leap over.

6

When we are old
and the planet is at war
we'll hold conversations
thigh-deep in the silken sea,

hands elaborate, fingers
ticking off the great idiocies,
the great simplicities.

Here are our tidemarked shorts,
stashed in the shade
of the beached boat,
our sandals companionable
on the shore.

Long after our lovers
have abandoned us
the water will stroke
us with its constant tears,

till we are salt-smooth
like pebbles, our contours
airbrushed by light.

Twice groomed
and twice mirrored,
at our feet
the little flattering fishes,
each one a flash of desire
in the silver eye of *Ilios*.